BIRMINGHAM'S RAILWAYS
A DECADE OF CHANGE

KRIS DAVIES

AMBERLEY

First published 2024

Amberley Publishing
The Hill, Stroud
Gloucestershire, GL5 4EP

www.amberley-books.com

Copyright © Kris Davies, 2024

The right of Kris Davies to be identified as
the Author of this work has been asserted in
accordance with the Copyrights, Designs and
Patents Act 1988.

ISBN 978 1 3981 1734 1 (print)
ISBN 978 1 3981 1735 8 (ebook)

British Library Cataloguing in Publication Data.
A catalogue record for this book is available from
the British Library.

Origination by Amberley Publishing.
Printed in the UK.

Contents

Introduction

The world we live in, especially in the twenty-first century, is always in a state of change. The British railway industry is certainly not immune to this, with new rolling stock arriving, services changing and new companies taking over passenger franchises on a regular basis.

One of these changes occurred in 2016 when West Midlands Trains took over from the previous West Midlands (and beyond) railway franchise holder London Midland. West Midlands Trains created two brands: West Midlands Railway for services in the West Midlands and London Northwestern Railway for services along the West Coast Main Line as far as Liverpool, as well as some other routes outside of the West Midlands.

West Midlands Trains is accountable to the Department for Transport and the West Midlands Rail Executive. In the West Midlands region, rail also falls under the purview of Transport for West Midlands. West Midlands Railway's brand was designed to fit in alongside the new brands for the West Midlands Metro tram network and buses.

In the years since the franchise change and new governance, the railway scene in the West Midlands has changed dramatically in a number of areas. The most notable change a passenger, or customer as they are termed these days, may notice is the West Midlands Railway branding rolled out to rolling stock, stations and publications including information screens. Unlike some of the other Train Operating Companies which have taken over franchises in recent years, West Midlands Railway have been thorough in establishing their brand across the network and now there are few traces of London Midland's brand remaining (London Northwestern Railway is another story that we will see later in this book).

Station upgrades and redevelopments have taken place including at the three key stations on the West Coast Main Line in the West Midlands: Birmingham New Street, Wolverhampton and Coventry. Upgrades and improvements have also taken place at a number of other stations across Birmingham and the West Midlands including improving accessibility and capacity.

One change that has been slow to come to fruition is new rolling stock, which was promised as long ago as 2017 when the franchise change took place. Train testing and the training of staff on the new trains was badly delayed by the Covid-19 pandemic. At the time of writing (early 2023) only a small number of the new trains promised have entered service, though the rest are due over the next couple of years.

The West Midlands Metro light rail network has probably seen the greatest number of changes over the last few years. Rebranded as part of Transport for West Midlands, the Metro has seen new rolling stock completely replacing the original fleet, a new livery and an extension into and across Birmingham city centre. Three more extensions are currently under construction.

The changes to the rail scene will be continuing in the future, mostly notably with the arrival of High Speed 2 in the late 2020s (or early 2030s as seems more likely). New stations at Curzon Street, next to Birmingham Moor Street, and at Birmingham Interchange near to Birmingham International will be built for the new high-speed services from London. One of the Midland Metro extensions will be to serve the new HS2 terminus. However, that is all a number of years away.

Before that a number of new stations are scheduled to open (or reopen) in the West Midlands in the early to mid-2020s and there are also plans to expand Moor Street and divert some New Street services there.

This book will cover Birmingham and the West Midlands railways from the mid-2010s to 2022, travelling line by line and visiting every station in the region. The area covered corresponds to the West Midlands Network's fare zone area, the only exception being the extremities of the Cross City Line, which are in Worcestershire and Staffordshire and are included for completion.

So, let us take a tour across Birmingham's railway network.

City Centre Stations

There are three large stations in Birmingham city centre. Before we venture out along the various lines in the Birmingham and West Midlands area, let us first have a look at these.

Birmingham New Street is the largest and busiest station in the region, and is one of the busiest railway stations outside of London. New Street is served by five different Train Operating Companies (TOCs), including Transport for Wales (TfW), which operates services from Birmingham to Wales (as far as Aberystwyth and Pwllheli) and also to Chester. TfW took over from Arriva Trains Wales in 2018 and is now publicly owned by the Welsh government. On 9 July 2020 TfW 158 825 stands at New Street.

Awarded the West Midlands railway franchise in 2007, London Midland operated local services in the West Midlands and services down the West Coast Main Line. When West Midlands Trains took over in 2017, the franchise was split into two separate identities: West Midlands Railway (WMR) and London Northwestern Railway (LNR), which operates between London Euston and Liverpool Lime Street (along with some other services outside of the scope of this book). On 12 September 2015 350 116 in London Midland livery has just arrived at New Street.

New Street is the Cross Country franchise's hub, the closest the company has to a home station (as unlike most Train Operating Companies it does not manage any railway stations itself, even stations where it is the only company to stop there). On 10 February 2022 a High Speed Train headed by 43 239 prepares to depart for the South West.

There are four variants of Class 350, part of Siemens Transportation's Desiro family of electric multiple units. The variants have a mixture of 2 by 2 and 2 by 3 seating. By 2016, all 350s built were in operation with London Midland, having been transferred from other companies such as TransPennine Express. All were then transferred to London Northwestern Railway. Nearly half of the fleet is due to be replaced by Class 730 units in the early 2020s. On 12 May 2012 London Midland 350 254 stands in the New Street sunshine.

During 2021 and 2022 Birmingham New Street underwent a full upgrade of its signalling system, replacing 1960s vintage signalling equipment and allowing for the operational closure of the Brutalist icon that is the New Street signal box. Each platform has been upgraded separately in turn to avoid disruption as much as possible, with the rest of the station operating as normal. Road-Railer 910166-6 stands at New Street on 9 August 2021.

On 20 June 2022, West Midlands Railway 170 517 arrives with a service from Shrewsbury. West Midlands Railway (WMR) have re-liveried all of their trains (to varying degrees) including stock like this one which was due for replacement within a few years. The 170s have been replaced by newly built Class 196s, which began entering service in October 2022. The 170s have been transferred to East Midlands Railway.

Birmingham New Street was upgraded as part of the Grand Central development which created a new concourse on top of the platforms (though the changes at platform level have been few and far between). New Street at platform level often retains a gloomy feel below the shiny shops above. On 16 December 2021 a variety of CrossCountry stock can be seen at New Street.

During leaf fall season, Network Rail's fleet of Rail Head Treatment Trains are hard at work criss-crossing the railway network cleaning the rails to try and avoid rail slippage. On 16 December 2022 DR98917 stands at New Street having ended one such trip.

As well as regularly scheduled services, Birmingham New Street, being at the literal heart of the railway network, is frequently visited by rail tours and excursions. West Coast 47 804 stands at New Street on 12 November 2019.

Avanti West Coast took over from Virgin Trains in 2019 and are the main operator at Birmingham New Street for services along the West Coast Main Line. Avanti West Coast Pendolino 390 156 stands at New Street on 18 January 2020.

As well as the electric Class 390s, diesel-powered Class 221 Super Voyagers are also used on West Coast Main Line services by Avanti West Coast. They are due to be replaced by the bi-mode Class 805 in the early 2020s. On 7 April 2021, and still in Virgin Trains livery, 221 106 stands at New Street.

On 23 February 2019, West Midlands Railway 170 511 stands at Birmingham New Street ready to depart with a service to Hereford. The Class 172s took over this route from Class 170s in 2020. The new Class 196 will take over by the mid-2020s.

A railtour visits Birmingham New Street on 26 September 2022 headed by 43 184 in British Rail InterCity livery.

On 8 September 2018, not long after West Midlands Trains took over from London Midland, 172 339 stands at Birmingham Moor Street, the city's second busiest station. This was a prototype livery for West Midlands Railway, which was only carried by this unit and was soon replaced by the definitive WMR livery, which is predominantly orange.

Birmingham Moor Street is managed by Chiltern Railways, who operate trains to London Marylebone (and sometimes as far as Kidderminster in the other direction). Christmas branded Driving Van Trailer 82302 stands at Moor Street on 22 December 2017. A Class 68 diesel locomotive is at the other end of the train ready to push it to the capital.

And here is the other end of one of Chiltern's expresses! On 26 July 2021, Chiltern 68 013 stands at Birmingham Moor Street having recently arrived with a service from London Marylebone. Around half of Chiltern services start and terminate from Moor Street; in peak hours trains can start/end from as far as Kidderminster.

On 17 November 2015, Chiltern 168 109 arrives at Birmingham Moor Street with a service from London Marylebone. Chiltern Railways are one of the longest-surviving railway franchise holders.

On the last day of London Midland operation (9 December 2017), 172 335 and 332 meet at Moor Street. The Class 172s operate between Worcester and Stratford-upon-Avon on what are often referred to as the Snow Hill Lines.

Birmingham Moor Street was opened by the Great Western Railway in 1909. It was restored in the early 2000s to reinstate its original GWR feel and the station has won a number of heritage awards. It is early on 9 November 2019 and the station (and city) is quiet, waiting for the busy Saturday to come.

A London Midland Class 172 stands at Moor Street on 17 May 2013. While Moor Street has retained its period feel, the station is surrounded by new developments including the Selfridges building. More is to come with the HS2 terminus being built at Curzon Street just a short walk away. There are plans to upgrade Moor Street in the future, which include adding two new platforms and switching East Midlands and South West services from New Street to Moor Street.

A variety of motive power stands at Moor Street's two-bay platforms on 23 April 2016. Direct Rail Services-liveried and Chiltern Railways-operated 68 009 heads a recently arrived express from London Marylebone. Chiltern 165 001 prepares to depart with a local service to Leamington Spa.

Early morning on 11 May 2017 on the Moor Street concourse. Unlike New Street's concourse, Moor Street's has not changed a great deal over the last few years. The station is frequently used as a filming location due to its 'period feel'.

Birmingham Snow Hill is the city centre's third major railway station. The original station was opened by the Great Western Railway in 1852 and was for a time a rival to New Street in size and services. The station went into a decline post-war and was finally closed and demolished in 1972. A new Snow Hill was built and opened in 1987 underneath a car park and offices, and the tunnel through to Moor Street reopened. On 9 July 2020, West Midlands Railway 172 220 waits for its next turn.

Until the rebranding of its stock could be completed, West Midlands Railway removed the London Midland stickers and replaced them with WMR ones. However, in the case of 170 634 at Birmingham Snow Hill on 27 December 2017, it is still waiting for its new Train Operating Company identity!

Chiltern-liveried 68 012 stands at the rear of this express bound for London Marylebone on 9 July 2020. Using Driving Van Trailers and Mark 3 coaching stock Chiltern began operating these locomotive-hauled expresses in 2010, firstly with Class 67s as motive power, changing to Class 68s in 2014. The expresses use Mark 3 coaching stock with a Driving Van Trailer at the other end.

A new entrance on Livery Street was opened at Snow Hill in 2011. More planned upgrades to the station include adding a fourth platform in the late 2020s and removing the car park above, replacing it with new offices. Snow Hill is managed by West Midlands Railway and served by them and Chiltern Railways.

West Midlands Railway 172 335 stands at Snow Hill on 10 August 2019. Next to the unit is an early example of a promotional poster by WMR, using the diamonds of the West Midlands Transport brand (which are supposed to form a 'WM') as an integral part of the design. These diamonds can also be seen in the vinyl wrap on the side of the 172. However, the WMR logo itself seems to have lost a diamond!

Another view of 172 339 in its prototypical West Midlands Railway livery seen at Snow Hill on 27 December 2017. The platforms at Snow Hill can be rather dingy and gloomy underneath the car park.

A comparison of liveries as Chiltern Railways 168 111 and London Midland 172 339 stand at Snow Hill on 7 August 2013.

Platform level at Snow Hill on 27 December 2017. West Midlands Railway branding has been applied to the signage and concrete pillars.

While work was ongoing improving Livery Street access at Snow Hill on 31 May 2014, London Midland 172 335 stands ready for its next duty.

Birmingham to Coventry

Leaving the city centre, we are now travelling along the West Coast Main Line towards Coventry.

Our first stop is Adderley Park, which is just outside the city centre. On 27 March 2021, London Northwestern Railway 350 239 departs with a Coventry-bound service. A mix of LNR and West Midlands Railway trains are used on this line.

A Virgin Trains Super Voyager 221 passes through Stechford on 17 October 2017. Most passing services will go on to New Street, though a branch line just south of the station allows for diversions through to Aston and up to Walsall and beyond. This diversion route is often used if there is engineering work or disruption on the Trent Valley branch of the West Coast Main Line.

Later the same day, London Midland 350 371 departs with a New Street-bound service. Stechford was the author's old trainspotting haunt in the early 1980s; back then though it was Class 86- and 87-hauled expresses passing through and Class 310s stopping on local services.

Stechford, like a number of stations in the West Midlands, has been upgraded to improve accessibility. A new footbridge and lifts were installed in 2020 along with other improvements to the station.

On 2 February 2019, London Northwestern Railway 350 107 departs Lea Hall bound for Birmingham. The train is in an early version of the LNR livery, with new stickers replacing the old London Midland ones. Otherwise the livery is largely unchanged. Unlike West Midlands Railway, LNR has not fully re-liveried all of its trains.

In late afternoon winter sunshine, West Midlands Railway 323 212 arrives at Lea Hall with a Birmingham-bound service on 2 February 2019.

Also on 2 February 2019, London Northwestern 350 256 arrives at Marston Green with a London Euston-bound service. The unit has simply had its London Midland stickers replaced by LNR ones, with the livery otherwise unchanged – a number of 350s have remained in this state. The seat moquette has also remained unchanged.

We are now approaching Birmingham Airport – Marston Green station is located next to the end of the runway, though if you have a flight you'll want to stay on the train for one more stop! On 2 February 2019, Arriva Trains Wales 158 838 passes through the station bound for Birmingham International.

A fully London Northwestern Railway-branded 350 130 arrives at Marston Green on 31 July 2022. The LNR brand is predominantly dark green and silver.

Birmingham International serves Birmingham Airport, the National Exhibition Centre and other local attractions. On the cold night of 20 December 2019 350 134 stands ready to depart.

West Midlands Railway Class 323s can also been seen at Birmingham International on local services, though back in October 2016 323 205 was in London Midland colours. The station is managed by Avanti West Coast.

Hampton-in-Arden served as Birmingham Airport's station until the construction of Birmingham International in the 1970s. This is why the station has platforms much longer than nowadays needed for local stopping services (parts of the platforms have now been fenced out of use). On 2 February 2019, a Virgin Trains Super Voyager passes through the station bound for London Euston.

On 2 February 2019, a Virgin Trains Pendolino passes through Hampton-in-Arden. The station was in the middle of its West Midlands Railway rebranding. The lampposts and handrails have been repainted in West Midlands Railway orange and grey but the signage is still London Midland!

London Northwestern Railway 350 116 (though still mostly in London Midland livery) arrives at Berkswell on 27 June 2020.

LNWR 350 116 departs Berkswell for London Euston. The new standard platform branding for West Midlands Railway managed stations can be seen. The orange area of the sign is used for local information or promoting local services, in this case direct trains to the airport.

We are now approaching Coventry. Tile Hill has been thoroughly West Midlands Railway branded. London Northwestern Railway 350 406 is seen on 7 July 2020.

Canley in Coventry's outskirts has these interesting lampposts which have been given the West Midlands Railway orange treatment. London Northwestern Railway 350 260 departs for Coventry on 3 April 2021.

Coventry is a major stop on the West Coast Main Line served by a number of companies including CrossCountry. On 3 June 2017, Super Voyager 221 141 is about to head down the line to Leamington Spa on its way to the south coast. Coventry is managed by Avanti West Coast, and before that Virgin Trains.

On 5 April 2021, London Northwestern Railway 350 401 arrives with a London Euston-bound service. The station was rebuilt between 2019 and 2022, including a new concourse, car park and footbridge. The new buildings, in a state of construction, can be seen in the background.

Virgin Trains 390 122 stands at Coventry on a London Euston-bound service on 3 June 2017.

Coventry Arena is included in the West Midlands Network as far as fare zones are concerned and therefore is included here. London Midland 153 366 arrives on 3 June 2017 with a Nuneaton-bound service. Coventry Arena was opened in 2016 to serve Coventry Stadium, known as the Ricoh Arena at the time of this photograph.

Birmingham to Wolverhampton

Now we head north along the West Coast Main Line from New Street to Wolverhampton.

On 10 September 2017, Arriva Trains Wales 158 826 passes through Smethwick Rolfe Street heading for New Street.

Smethwick Galton Bridge is a highly important station in the West Midlands. It is the only station that offers direct interchange between lines heading to and from New Street and Snow Hill. On 7 April 2021, London Northwestern Railway 350 117 stands with a northbound service.

In London Midland days, 323 210 arrives at Smethwick Galton Bridge on 11 March 2017. The photograph can be compared with the one above; the difference, something as simple as painting lampposts orange, can be startling!

On 31 December 2022 London Northwestern Railway 350 123 arrives at Dudley Port with a Wolverhampton-bound service. The station is not too close to the centre of Dudley, though a future West Midlands Metro extension will bring the (light) railway into Dudley's heart.

On a gloomy 31 December 2022, London Northwestern Railway 350 240 arrives at Tipton with a Birmingham-bound service.

On the border of Wolverhampton is Coseley station. London Northwestern Railway 350 242 departs on 28 August 2020.

Coseley's modern station facilities, including this waiting room, sit well alongside the West Midlands Railway's branding.

Wolverhampton station is one of the region's main stations. On 12 September 2015, two London Midland 350s, 128 and 251, stand alongside each other. 251 is bound for New Street; 128 is heading north.

On 10 August 2022, Avanti West Coast Pendolino 390 047 stands at Wolverhampton. Behind the unit an interesting variation of the standard West Midlands Railway station nameboard design can be seen.

Wolverhampton has received a major redevelopment including this new station front, which opened in 2022. In the foreground are the tracks for a West Midlands Metro extension due to open in mid-2023.

In late 2022 the first of the new rolling stock ordered for West Midlands Railway finally entered service. The Class 196 replaced Class 170s on services to Shrewsbury to start with and later on other diesel-hauled services too. WMR 196 110 is seen at Wolverhampton on 10 November 2022.

Birmingham to Walsall

Now we head north from Birmingham New Street to Walsall.

Although it looks somewhat run-down and unwelcoming these days, Duddeston is Birmingham's oldest railway station. It was the original city terminus opening in 1837 as Vauxhall for services on the Grand Junction Railway from the north. On 22 July 2017, London Midland 323 241 departs with a Walsall-bound service. The station is also the first stop on the northern half of the Cross City Line, which we will explore later on.

On 6 July 2022, London Northwestern Railway 350 103 arrives at Aston with a Birmingham-bound service. The Cross City Line branches off of the line to Walsall just past the end of the platforms.

On a wet 15 February 2020, West Midlands Railway 323 202 departs Witton. The station is the nearest to Aston Villa's football ground and therefore is busy (along with Aston station) on match days.

Perry Barr station was rebuilt in 2022 as part of transport improvements to prepare the region for hosting the Commonwealth Games. The main stadium for the games was close to Perry Barr station, which is seen on 3 July 2022 just before the games began. London Northwestern Railway 350 254 departs with a Walsall-bound service.

The exterior of Perry Barr station was completely changed to this 'copper box' design, which has proven controversial to some, though is certainly 'on brand'!

The heavens have opened on 15 February 2020, but West Midlands Railway 323 202 arrives at Hamstead without a care!

The two identities of West Midlands Trains side by side. London Northwestern Railway 350 372 arrives at Tame Bridge Parkway on 13 July 2019 meeting West Midlands Railway-branded 323 211. This is one of a number of parkway stations across the West Midlands network.

Approaching Walsall, first we reach Bescot Stadium located next to a Bescot yard and depot. The station is named after Walsall's football ground, which is nearby. On 28 December 2016, London Midland 323 201 departs for Walsall.

Due to the adjacent yard and TMD, Bescot Stadium is a good location in the West Midlands for seeing freight services. On 8 August 2021, GB Railfreight 66 786 leads a train through the station.

On a cold 20 December 2020, London Northwestern Railway 350 370 has just arrived at Walsall. Soon it will head back to New Street.

An unusual view of a London Midland 323 221 on 12 May 2017. It will soon depart for Wolverhampton via New Street.

North of Walsall the Chase Line continues on to Rugeley in Staffordshire. However, the first two stations in Bloxwich are in the West Midlands Network area. This view at Bloxwich on 30 March 2021 clearly shows the West Midlands Railway station nameboard variation if there is no local information to convey.

Bloxwich North is the last station we will cover on this line, though London Northwestern Railway 350 405 will continue on to Rugeley Trent Valley on 30 March 2021.

Cross City North

Now we head north on the Cross City Line.

At Aston the Cross City Line branches off from the line to Walsall. Aston is used by football fans going to Villa Park and is very busy on match days. On 6 July 2022, West Midlands Railway 323 240 departs north.

West Midlands Railway 323 211 prepares to depart Aston on 13 July 2019. Aston is a junction station with lines diverging from the main at both sides of the station.

On 9 August 2021, West Midlands Railway 323 215 arrives at Aston under heavy cloud.

Gravelly Hill is the home of Gravelly Hill Interchange, which is of course more commonly known as the Spaghetti Junction. Despite being within earshot, the motorway junction is not visible from the railway station, although the Cross City Line does pass underneath it after departing Aston for Gravelly Hill. On 15 March 2014, London Midland 323 204 is seen heading north.

As with other stations which are now managed by West Midlands Railway, Gravelly Hill has been repainted in a grey and orange livery. However, unlike most of the other stations on the northern half of the Cross City Line, Gravelly Hill has retained its original London North Western Railway (LNWR) booking office. The station is in a cutting; the route to the next station, Erdington, is uphill.

On 18 October 2015, London Midland 323 215 stands at Erdington with a southbound service. As the station was on an embankment the original station buildings and platforms were made from wood due to weight and concerns about subsidence. However, all of these were replaced when the line was electrified in 1992.

During the leaf fall season, to help with the problem of slippery rails, Rail Head Treatment Trains (RHTT) are a common sight as they run to and from across the network, especially in areas with inclines, such as the Cross City Line North where adhesion can be an issue at the best of times. Windhoff Multi-Purpose Vehicle DR98959 heads north through Erdington cleaning the rails as it goes, also on 18 October 2015.

The Cross City Line North is a diversion route for CrossCountry trains between Tamworth and Birmingham New Street, which would usually travel via Water Orton. At weekends some services are run on this route to help drivers maintain their route knowledge. Empty coach stock movements from the Alstom depot near Burton-on-Trent also use the Cross City Line to reach New Street. On 17 August 2021, a CrossCountry High Speed Train heads through Chester Road bound for New Street.

Chester Road is named after the A452 Chester Road, which the railway passes over. Like many stations on the line, Chester Road's original LNWR buildings were lost during electrification. The waiting room was saved, however, and is now at Market Bosworth on the Battlefield Line. On 7 August 2019, West Midlands Railway 323 209 prepares to continue its journey north.

Some examples of branding outlast others. Chester Road's bridge (which crosses the actual Chester Road) still displays NetworkWM branding from before the advent of Transport West Midlands. Erdington's bridge also continues to display this now obsolete branding.

West Midlands Railway 323 204 departs north from Chester Road on 27 June 2020. Chester Road is one of a number of stations on the Cross City Line which has a large free car park for the use of park and ride passengers, including the author!

When London Midland's franchise ended in 2017, and West Midlands Railway (part of West Midlands Trains) took over, a new look was applied to the railway fleet inside and out. On a 323 standing at Chester Road the new moquette style applied to the seating can be seen – the design is based on the West Midlands Railway logo and using the grey and orange colour scheme also applied to stations. A green variation is carried by some London Northwestern Railway trains. A blue version is carried by the West Midlands Metro.

London Midland 323 210 stands at Wylde Green with a southbound service on 4 December 2016. As with Chester Road, the original LNWR wooden buildings have long gone, corrugated iron shelters protecting customers from the elements – though most of the platform area offers no protection at all.

Sutton Coldfield, which was opened by the LNWR in 1862, was the line's original terminus before the line was extended to Lichfield. The station is a somewhat grander affair than most on the line, the station retaining its original LNWR buildings. However, the station has lost the bay platform, goods yard and turntable it once had.

London Midland 323 214 stands in the winter sunshine at Sutton Coldfield on 4 December 2016. The Class 323s were built by Hunslet TPL in the early 1990s for the Cross City Line and for services to Manchester Airport in the north. The WMR fleet will be replaced by the Class 730; some will be transferred to join Northern's 323 fleet.

On 2 November 2019, West Midlands Railway 323 216 stands at Four Oaks with an early morning service to Lichfield Trent Valley. When the Cross City Line was launched in 1978, Four Oaks was the original northern terminus. Half of the trains on the route still terminate at Four Oaks (usually services which have originated from Redditch).

An unusual view of a West Midlands Railway 323 standing on Four Oak's bay platform on 2 November 2019 before it heads south to Redditch via Birmingham. Although Four Oaks has lost its original LNWR station building, it retains the original waiting room and canopies on the station's island platform.

Butlers Lane is the youngest station on the northern half of the Cross City Line, having been opened by British Railways in 1957 to serve new housing developments to the north of Sutton Coldfield. Opened as a halt on a temporary basis, the station originally had a wooden hut for a ticket office. This was replaced by a brick building in 1991. West Midlands Railway 323 202 arrives with a southbound service on 1 September 2018.

Blake Street is on the West Midlands/Staffordshire border and is the last station in the West Midlands ticket zone. The station is named after the road which passes to the north of the station (and where the county border is). On 22 July 2017, London Midland 323 204 heads north and into Staffordshire.

Shenstone was opened by the LNWR in 1884. The station retains its impressive original building and canopy. However, the opposite platform has the rather less aesthetically pleasing and ubiquitous bus shelter-type accommodation for customers (as they must be called these days!). The station is seen on 13 January 2018 with London Midland green instead of West Midlands Railway orange for the railings.

Two London Midland 323s await coupling up at Lichfield City on 11 February 2017. The unit on the left had suffered an electrical failure and was going to be coupled up to return it to Soho Depot in Birmingham for repairs. Nowadays, Lichfield City is only served by the Cross City Line but once also had services to Walsall and Dudley.

London Midland 323 210 stands at Lichfield City on 11 February 2017. North of the station the line will continue to the Cross City Line's terminus at Lichfield's other railway station.

London Midland 323 210 stands at Lichfield Trent Valley on 11 February 2017 before it makes its journey back to Birmingham through the light snow. This is the terminus of the Cross City Line – the railway does continue north beyond this point, although it is not electrified, so the 323 will not be going any further! The station's two other platforms serve the West Coast Main Line.

Cross City South

Returning to the city centre, we now head south on the Cross City Line towards Worcestershire.

Just outside the very centre of the city, Five Ways serves Broad Street, Birmingham's nightlife centre and a major business area. In 2022 it gained an interchange with the Midlands Metro, which was extended to Edgbaston Village. West Midlands Railway 323 213 arrives on 24 August 2020 with a southbound service.

University is located between the adjoining campuses of the University of Birmingham and the Queen Elizabeth Hospital in Edgbaston. On 21 September 2019, West Midlands Railway 323 205 arrives with a Birmingham-bound service.

University was opened in 1978 and has been in need of a major upgrade for some time. This finally began in 2019 with the intention of opening the new station ready for the Commonwealth Games (some events being held at the university campus). However, the station was not finished in time and at the time of writing in early 2023 work is continuing. On 6 November 2022, West Midlands Railway 323 209 arrives between the new station buildings still in a state of incompletion.

The new station is much larger than the existing University with large buildings on both sides linked by a footbridge walkway. The new station also has much more extensive canopies and wider platforms than the original one.

University is also served by some CrossCountry services, though on 6 November 2022 Super Voyager 221 133 passes through bound for New Street. Although the new station is not yet open, passengers can still take advantage of the new canopies.

West Midlands Railway 323 216 departs Selly Oak for New Street on 7 January 2022. The station was opened in 1876 but is now completely unrecognisable having been completely rebuilt in 1978. The station has gained a new free car park in recent years and is one of the Cross City Line's park and ride stations.

Bournville is adjacent to Cadbury's famous chocolate factory. To celebrate this, the station has been painted in Cadbury's purple and not the standard West Midlands Railway orange and grey. On 8 August 2021, WMR 323 207 departs southwards.

On 7 January 2022, West Midlands Railway 323 215 arrives at Kings Norton with a Birmingham-bound service. The station once had four platforms but the central island platform has remained unused for some time. The island platform could be brought back to use under plans to reopen the Camp Hill line in the mid-2020s.

On a gloomy 20 March 2021, West Midlands Railway 323 241 arrives at Northfield with a Longbridge-bound service. Like Kings Norton, Northfield also once had an island platform. The island platform is now rather derelict, though is host to some artworks.

A West Midlands Railway 323 has arrived at Longbridge on 4 January 2022. The unit will continue on to either Redditch or Bromsgrove. After leaving Longbridge, it leaves the West Midlands and enters Worcestershire. A few Cross City services terminate at this station.

Barnt Green is a junction station, the line heading off down to Redditch on the right. On 17 March 2019, a CrossCountry High Speed Train led by 43 378 is about to head down the famous (or is that infamous?) Lickey incline on its way to the South West.

On 24 March 2018, West Midlands Railway 323 215 departs Alvechurch on its way to Redditch. The unit is still wearing its London Midland livery apart from the logos, which have been covered over. The Cross City is single track from Barnt Green to Redditch, though a passing loop was built at Alvechurch in 2014 to enable an increased train frequency.

Redditch is the end of the line for this branch of the Cross City. On 4 March 2017, London Midland 323 214 stands ready for the return trip back to Birmingham. The railway line once used to continue south to Evesham, though this stretch closed in the 1960s.

In 2016, Bromsgrove station was rebuilt and the Cross City Line electrification extended down from Barnt Green in 2018. The Cross City Line was extended to the town down the Lickey incline. On 15 December 2018, West Midlands Railway 170 635 stands with a Hereford-bound service.

On 15 December 2018, West Midlands Railway 323 204 stands at Bromsgrove, the end of the Cross City Line. Even if the unit wanted to it could not go much further as this is the limit of electrification – for now at least.

Birmingham to Whitlocks End

We will now switch to the Snow Hill lines and head south from Birmingham Moor Street to Whitlocks End.

The first stop on the line is Bordesley, which is the runt of the litter when it comes to Birmingham's railway stations. It only has one scheduled train stop a week (on Saturdays), though it does have more services on match days at the nearby St Andrew's football ground of Birmingham City Football Club. On 27 June 2021, West Midlands Railway 172 214 departs after depositing passengers on the only train for that week. Only two passengers disembarked, including the author! The station's future is in doubt as it may close if some New Street services are moved to an expanded Moor Street.

On 22 June 2017, London Midland 172 342 arrives at Small Heath. The station was opened by the Great Western Railway in 1863 near to the famous BSA factory. How often the Peaky Blinders used Small Heath station is unfortunately unknown.

Tyseley is a great example of surviving Great Western Railway architecture with its platform buildings and canopies, though the station could do with a bit of tender love and care, especially with a paintbrush! On 25 June 2016, a CrossCountry service heads through. Next to Tyseley station is one of West Midlands Railway's main motive power depots, as well as the location of Birmingham Tyseley Locomotive Works.

After Tyseley the line towards Stratford-upon-Avon via Whitlocks End splits away from the Chiltern Main Line. First stop is Spring Road, which opened in 1908 in a fairly rural location as a platform to serve a small number of cottages. The station is now deep within Birmingham's southern suburbs. On 5 September 2020, West Midlands Railway 172 344 departs with a service to Whitlocks End.

London Midland 172 214 stands at Hall Green with a Stratford-bound service on 11 March 2017. Stations on this route have been painted a Great Western Railway-style brown and beige, a colour scheme that has survived the change to West Midlands Railway (although the signage has been changed).

London Midland 172 220 stands at Yardley Wood on 11 March 2017. We are now on the edge of Birmingham and about to enter Solihull. As with most stations on this line, Yardley Wood retains its original GWR station buildings.

On 17 November 2018, a de-branded West Midlands Railway 172 218 prepares to depart Shirley in Solihull. The unit is framed by a new set of lifts and a footbridge. A number of stations on what is now called the Shakespeare Line have received such an accessibility upgrade. The original name of the line is the North Warwickshire Line, named after a local fox hunt.

West Midlands Railway 172 344 stands at Whitlocks End on 28 June 2021. The station is the terminating point of two thirds of the services on the line, the other services continuing on to Stratford-upon-Avon.

On 11 March 2017, West Midlands Railway 172 214 stands at Whitlocks End with a Birmingham-bound service. The service earlier terminated at the station and will begin the return journey 'wrong road' before crossing over just past the Birmingham end of the station platforms.

Birmingham to Stourbridge

We now head from Birmingham Snow Hill to Stourbridge Junction.

The first stop is Jewellery Quarter. As with many stations on the line, it is served by both West Midlands Railway and Chiltern Railway, though managed by the former. In most cases Chiltern only provides a limited service in peak hours. On 11 March 2017, Chiltern 168 005 is passing through heading for Birmingham Snow Hill.

Heading into the Black Country, on 11 March 2017 London Midland 172 337 arrives at The Hawthorns. The station is named after the nearby ground of West Bromwich Albion Football Club. Both Jewellery Quarter and The Hawthorns railway stations also have platforms for the Midlands Metro.

We have seen Smethwick Galton Bridge on the Birmingham–Wolverhampton line already. The station also has two platforms serving the Snow Hill lines. On 5 January 2023, West Midlands Railway 172 213 departs heading towards Stourbridge Junction. The two Birmingham–Wolverhampton platforms are on the lower level. The station is named after Galton Bridge, which spans the canal next to the station and can be seen from the platforms.

We are now in Oldbury, Langley Green being the next stop on the line. West Midlands Railway 172 219 departs on 27 December 2019.

On 27 December 2019, West Midlands Railway 172 219 arrives at Rowley Regis with a Birmingham-bound service. The Class 172 was built for London Midland, Chiltern Railways and London Overground in the early 2010s and at the time it was planned to be the last diesel multiple units to be built for the British railway network (though newer units such as the Class 196 have since been built). The entire 172 fleet is now operated by West Midlands Railway.

On 31 December 2022, West Midlands Railway 172 214 arrives at Old Hill with a Birmingham-bound service.

On 31 December 2022, West Midlands Railway 172 332 departs Old Hill with a Kidderminster-bound service. Some services on this line terminate at Stourbridge Junction, though others continue onwards as far as Worcester.

On 31 March 2021, West Midlands Railway 172 219 departs Cradley Heath heading for Stourbridge Junction.

On 9 July 2020, West Midlands Railway 172 006 departs Lye. This is one of the ex-London Overground Class 172s which were transferred to West Midlands Railway in 2019 after the electrification of the Gospel Oak–Barking Line left them surplus to requirements.

On a wet 3 October 2020, West Midlands Railway 172 219 stands at Stourbridge Junction. Although some Snow Hill services terminate here, this train will continue on to Worcester Foregate Street.

Stourbridge Junction is the home of the unique Class 139s, powered by flywheel and diesel engines, which operate the shuttle service down to Stourbridge Town. A small depot is located next to Stourbridge Junction station for the two units which operate on the line. In London Midland livery 139 002 arrives at Stourbridge Junction after making the short trip up from Stourbridge Town on 28 January 2017.

On 4 October 2020, WMR 139 001 stands at the tiny railway terminus that is Stourbridge Town. The two Class 139s have gained a mostly purple version of the West Midlands Railway livery. Before the Class 139s entered service in 2009, the branch was operated by a Class 153 single-car unit, and before that a first-generation diesel bubble car.

On 28 January 2017, London Midland 139 002 stands at Stourbridge Town ready to make the short trip uphill to the junction. The unit will use energy stored by its flywheel, harvested while travelling downhill from Stourbridge Junction (from the brakes), to augment the small diesel engine for the return journey uphill.

Birmingham to Dorridge

As we saw earlier, after Tyseley the line to Stratford via Whitlocks End splits off from the Chiltern Main Line. Now we will continue along the main line from Tyseley to Dorridge.

The first stop on the main line after Tyseley is Acocks Green. On 5 September 2020, West Midlands Railway 172 220 is preparing to depart for Birmingham. As with a number of other stations on the Snow Hill Lines, Acocks Green has gained lifts for step-free access to the platforms over the last few years. The lift is accessed via the car park, not the main station building, which is on a bridge over the line.

At first glance this looks like a Chiltern Railways 172 departing Olton. However, this is one of the four Chiltern Class 172s which were transferred to West Midlands Railway to strengthen the latter's fleet. On 13 November 2021, 172 101 still wore Chiltern Railway's livery apart from the Chiltern logos which had been replaced by WMRs. The unit has now been fully re-liveried in WMR colours.

The Chiltern Main Line sees a good deal of freight traffic mostly from Birmingham Freightliner Depot, which is just outside of the city centre. On 10 June 2017, Freightliner's 70 015 leads a container train through Olton.

Solihull station is managed by Chiltern Railways not West Midlands Railway. On 14 September 2019, Chiltern 168 003 pauses with a service to London Marylebone. This unit is one of a small number of Class 168 Clubmans built with Networker-type cab fronts.

Solihull is served by both Chiltern and West Midlands Railway. On 14 September 2019, the latter's 172 331 departs with a Birmingham-bound service. As with Acocks Green and Olton, Solihull has a single-island platform. A disused former platform (which is now a buddleia and weed plantation) can be seen on the left.

Steps up to the platform level at Solihull seen on 16 November 2021. The station also has lifts for step-free access. The station was rebuilt in the 1930s when the line between Lapworth and Olton was quadrupled by the GWR. The station had a pair of island platforms but only one of these remains in use.

Widney Manor was a later GWR addition to the line, opening in 1899. Unlike the other stations on the line, Widney Manor has been completely rebuilt in recent times. On 26 August 2020, West Midlands Railway 172 341 departs for Dorridge.

On 26 August 2020, Chiltern Railways 168 217 passes through Widney Manor with a Birmingham Moor Street-bound service. Most services at the station are provided by West Midlands Railway; Chiltern services only stop a few times in the early evening.

Dorridge marks the edge of West Midlands region operations, though some West Midlands Railway trains will continue on to Stratford-upon-Avon and Leamington Spa from here. On 10 March 2018, WMR 172 335 stands on platform 3, which is used by terminating WMR services. The driver has departed his cab and is now heading for the other end of the train – he will soon be driving it back to Birmingham.

Dorridge is managed by Chiltern Railways, as with Birmingham Moor Street and Solihull. One of the company's trains, 168 106, departs bound for London Marylebone on 10 March 2018.

Dorridge, as it is managed by Chiltern Railways, carries that company's branding and colours on station signs and station fittings. The orange of West Midlands Railway stations is instead a pale blue here!

West Midlands Metro

Of all the railways in Birmingham and the West Midlands, the Midlands Metro light rail network is the one which has seen the greatest number of changes over the past decade. The network has expanded from a rather out-of-the-way line between Birmingham Snow Hill and Wolverhampton into a much more visible city centre crossing network.

The new Birmingham terminus of the line is Edgbaston Village, which opened in mid-2022, seen here on 13 August of that year.

A major feature of the Metro extension to Edgbaston Village was that the line now passes along the nightlife centre of Birmingham – Broad Street. However, on the somewhat quieter early Saturday morning, tram number 46 passes along the road on 24 December 2022.

West Midlands Metro uses a blue colour scheme with similar design elements to West Midlands Railway such as in the logo and moquette, as can be seen on this view inside a tram at Edgbaston Village on 13 August 2022.

Sharing Broad Street with a National Express West Midlands bus, tram 36 heads up on 13 August 2022. This stretch of the Midlands Metro line is battery powered, though in a short distance the pantograph will be raised again.

Library stop was the Metro's terminus from 2019 until 2022. The stop serves the City of Birmingham Library and Symphony Hall. Tram 47 is seen on 24 December 2022 about to head up Broad Street.

To pass through the architecturally sensitive area of Birmingham Town Hall and Victoria Square, the trams were fitted with battery packs in 2019 to remove the need for overhead wiring. With the Town Hall in the background, tram 18 heads down towards New Street on 23 December 2019.

The Metro was extended to Birmingham New Street and the Grand Central shopping centre above the station in 2016. This stop served as the terminus until 2019. Tram 21 stands at Grand Central on 23 February 2019. It is soon to begin the return journey to Wolverhampton.

The city centre terminus of the Metro used to be at Birmingham Snow Hill but a stop on Bull Street now serves as the interchange stop for Snow Hill. On 29 June 2022, tram 44 arrives with a terminating service.

A Metro tram stands at the Bull Street stop before continuing on to New Street. The batteries that enable travel through the wireless section of the line past the Town Hall can be seen atop the front section of the tram.

The original rolling stock for the Midlands Metro, which opened in 1999, was the Ansaldo Breda T-69, number 10 of which can be seen approaching the then terminus at Birmingham Snow Hill on 7 August 2013. They were replaced by the CAF-built Urbos 3 tram in 2015. The fleet is now being augmented with the similar Urbos 100.

Snow Hill no longer has a direct connection to the Midland Metro – Bull Street and St Chad's stops are both a short walk away. On 9 June 2020, a Metro train passes the platforms at Snow Hill while West Midlands Railway 172 220 stands waiting for its next duty.

St Chad's tram stop is alongside the ends of the platforms of Birmingham Snow Hill but no easy way to transfer to the main line station exists – a short walk to the station's entrances is needed instead. On 2 January 2023 tram 34 departs for Bull Street.

Tram 42 arrives at St Paul's stop on 10 October 2022 with a Birmingham-bound service. St Paul's is one of the stops that serves the famous Birmingham Jewellery Quarter.

The Jewellery Quarter stop is one of a number of tram stops that is adjacent to a 'heavy' rail station. On 7 August 2021, tram 26 prepares to depart heading for Wolverhampton.

On 3 October 2022, tram 43 arrives at Soho Benson Road with a Birmingham-bound service. The tram stop was built on the site of Soho & Winson Green railway station, which closed in 1972. Much of the Midland Metro original line reused the Birmingham Snow Hill to Wolverhampton Low Level railway line, which closed to passengers in 1972.

This tram is in the pre-West Midlands Metro pink and white livery. Also notice the Network WM logo on the nose of the tram and the tram stop's nameboard. On 11 March 2017, tram 17 passes one of its friends at The Hawthorns stop. This stop is adjacent to The Hawthorns railway station.

In the current West Midlands Metro blue livery, tram 28 arrives with a Wolverhampton-bound service at The Hawthorns on 3 January 2023.

On 3 October 2022, tram 31 departs Trinity Way stop in West Bromwich with a Wolverhampton-bound service. This is one of a number of tram stops in West Bromwich.

On 3 October 2022, tram 42 departs West Bromwich Central stop with a Wolverhampton-bound service. The tram stop was built on the site of West Bromwich railway station, which closed in 1972.

Loxdale tram stop is on the edge of Wolverhampton. On a cold morning tram 38 arrives with a Birmingham-bound service on 21 December 2022.

Wolverhampton St George's is the terminus of the Midland Metro, though an extension to Wolverhampton railway station is currently (in early 2023) under construction and due to open later in the year. On 19 January 2023, tram 38 arrives with a service from Birmingham.

The Future and the Past

The changes will continue into the next decade. New rolling stock is now finally making its long-delayed appearance on the railways of Birmingham and the West Midlands.

The Class 730, part of the Bombardier (now Alstom) Aventra family of multiple units, will be taking over from West Midlands Railway 323s and some London Northwestern Railway 350s in the early to mid-2020s. WMR 730 005 stands at Crewe on 14 February 2022 after a test run up the West Coast Main Line.

West Midlands Railway 730 005 pauses at Lichfield Trent Valley on a test run on 1 February 2022. As with the Class 196 diesel multiple unit, the WMR 730s are sporting a more vivid orange than legacy units like the 323s and 172s.

The new face of diesel units for West Midlands Railway is the Class 196, which began entering service in late 2022 on services between Birmingham and Shrewsbury, replacing Class 170s. On 10 November 2022, 196 110 stands at Birmingham New Street before a service to Shrewsbury.

The early 2020s have seen West Midlands Railway operate various extra units from elsewhere on the network to plug the gaps in their fleet due to delays with the Class 196s. 170 506 is an East Midlands Railway (EMR) unit which was loaned to WMR for a short period. The unit is in the new EMR livery but with WMR logos! The unit is seen at Shrewsbury on 1 March 2022. As the Class 196s entered service these EMR 170s returned home.

With the Class 323's time on with West Midlands Railway finally coming to an end, 323 221 was repainted into Centro Regional Railways livery, celebrating their first livery operating in the West Midlands for British Rail in 1994. It is seen here at Chester Road on 31 January 2023. Some, though not all, of the West Midlands Railway 323s will be heading north to join the Northern fleet of 323s as the 730s take over in the coming years.